GHOSTS, S
AND
THINGS THAT GO BUMP IN THE NIGHT

To my gorgeous wife,
Dawn.

Forever and always.

Preface

It's a bright spring day as I look out of the window, I have Spotify playing and I'm in a reflective mood. I can't believe 55 years have passed so quickly. When I look back over my life I realise how lucky I have been to witness the impossible and implausible. I have met many wonderful people on my path who have both inspired me, taught me and become good friends.

Let me tell you a bit about myself.

Many years have passed and I have walked down many paths since I first began questioning life's mysteries. It was over forty years ago that a rather shy boy, different from other children, I was happy in my own thoughts and spent many hours just enjoying my own company. While most of my friends were discovering football, girls and smoking I had a "Eureka" moment.

It came about after buying a second-hand copy of Chariots of the Gods by Eric von Daniken at a local jumble sale my mother frequented looking for bargains. It leapt out at me from the bookstall and as soon as I arrived home I read it from cover to cover. That one book set me on a pathway to investigate, learn and discover many unexplained things about the world we live in.

It sparked my interest in UFOs and Aliens, ancient technology's and civilisation's, magic, witchcraft, the supernatural and much, much more. But more than that, it made me think, it made me question and it sent me on a lifelong search for answers that continues to this day. Those far off days were full of discovery, of magic and wonder as I went from one jumble sale to the next looking for books on the supernatural, the paranormal, anything that would give me nuggets of gold. I became a walking question mark asking many questions; why are we here? Is there a God? Is there reincarnation? Are UFOs/Aliens real? Is there life on other planets? What are Ghosts?

I felt what can best be described as an inner calling. It was as though I knew something deep inside my soul but couldn't remember what it was but I just knew there was more to life than this. I had what you could call visions as a boy and I also suffered nightmares and sleep paralysis. Years later I realised I was having my first glimpses of the unseen world(s) that surround us.

I used to think a lot, an awful lot to be honest and I still do to this day. I am very analytical; being a Virgo I question everything. I vividly remember that I would awake in the night frozen with fear as the atmosphere in my bedroom seemed to change, to become very still almost as though it was charged with some sort of energy or electricity. Lying in bed I used to hear a sort of clicking noise as though someone was walking through the woods and the old, dead twigs were breaking beneath their feet. I would become paralysed with fear, sweating, I tried to cry out but couldn't as the noises came closer and louder, eventually I would yell out "MUMMMMM" and my mother would come rushing in the room explaining that I had a nightmare.

On other occasions in the early hours of the morning I would dream such vivid dreams I could remember every detail. Often in colour, I would write them down, something I do to this day. They are so real I feel I am sometimes witnessing some unseen world as an observer. I used to see strange shapes and colours floating around my bedroom as though they were floating in water, strange creatures not unlike fish from the depths of the ocean, lights, and other weird stuff. My mum though I imagined it or dreamt it, but I didn't, it was very real to me.

I also found that I had what today we would call as Past Life Recall. I could remember things from our distant past and see them in my minds eyes as though I was watching a television screen of moving images. One of my earliest "visions" was of the world being like an onion, made up of many layers and dimensions all co-existing beside and inside each other but none being aware of the dimension next to them. I believe this is what science and modern string theory is just discovering today, that there are many dimensions, and many of us are living our lives in different dimensions simultaneously having differing experiences at the same time.

So here I am at 55, writing this from memory and my extensive diaries, everything you read really happened and I witnessed it personally. I can't explain it and I don't have all the answers just pieces of the puzzle of this thing called "Life"

I consider myself an explorer of the unknown and like all explorers I have travelled many paths, some dead ends and some providing answers to my questions. My early interests lead me into witchcraft, The Rosicrucian's, The Knights Templars, magic (Both of the entertainment kind and occult kind), meditation, healing, tarot reading, spiritualism, mediumship, clairvoyance, martinism, mysticism, hypnotherapy, psychology, philosophy, consciousness and spirituality.

Today I still question, I still search, and I work as a Healer and Psychic Medium from my home in Kent. I hope this very brief glimpse into part of my world will inspire you to search for yourselves and I sincerely hope your search proves as fruitful and wonderful as mine has been.

May light shine upon your path and love illuminate your heart.

Ian Broadmore 02/03/2015

CONTENTS

The Hellfire Caves

In the summer of 1992 I visited the Hellfire Caves in West Wycombe with a group of friends that had an interest in the paranormal. The chalk caves were allegedly the setting of the infamous "Hell Fire Club" of Sir Francis Dashwood and extend for a quarter a mile underground. As you descend deeper into the cavers there are various passages and rooms and further down you cross the river Styx which according to mythology separated the world of the living from the underworld.

Eventually you reach the inner temple and are approximately 300 feet beneath St Lawrence's church. On the way, you pass through the banqueting hall which is about 500 foot from the main entrance and has a large 40ft dome shaped ceiling. This chamber is circular and designed like a compass with four recesses set into the walls, clearly symbolic of the four cardinal points of North, South, East, and West.

It was in this chamber that I sensed something. This room although named the "banqueting hall" I believe was used for ritualistic purposes in the past, as it was laid out in the form of a magical circle with the four cardinal points representing the four elements of Earth in the North quarter, Air in the East, Fire in the South and Water in the West.

I saw what I can only describe as a griffin that was pacing up and down, this mythical creature was some sort of guardian or protector. One of my friends who was also extremely psychic could see it as well. After a while it just faded from view and we continued downwards into the inner temple chamber of the caves.

In this small chamber were several small statues of the Goddess Venus, Peter, my friend, saw the apparition of a lady and Eleanor witnessed a ghostly hand caressing the statue of Venus. After we returned to the car park we sat down and chatted about experiences in the Hellfire caves. We all felt that they had been used in the distant part for some sort of Goddess worship and magical rituals.

There have been reports of chanting being heard from the inner temple and stones being thrown at people by unseen hands. Many sightings are of a ghostly figure of a young lady that lost her life in the banqueting hall.

Alchemical drawing of the mythical Griffin that was
seen as an energy form in the Hellfire caves.

In Search for Aleister Crowley's Ghost

In the late 90s I lived in St Leonards on Sea in East Sussex. This seaside town has a long history of the occult and supernatural and seems to draw those of that particular ilk.

At that time, I was involved in white witchcraft and other mystical activities. Along with my then wife I was a member of a white Wiccan group in Dorking, Surrey. Although we lived in a modern three bedroom detached house just off The Ridge area of Hastings we had lots of paranormal occurrences.

On more than one occasion I witnessed a hooded figure of a tall man on the stairs, wearing what looked like a robe of some sort but with the hood pulled up. My wife on another occasion witnessed a dog with red eyes in one of the children's bedrooms and my mother refused to stay the night ever again after her experience.

My mother came to stay one weekend and slept in my daughter's room as we put my daughter in with my son. At about 2am in the morning my mum screamed out, I rushed in the room and she was convinced she saw someone wearing a robe standing by her bed. I frequently used to see a pale blue light in the lounge that was there one minute and gone the next. My young daughter also used to experience conversations with some imaginary person in her bedroom.

However, the house had a good warm feeling about it and there was no previous history. As it was a new build I do not know what previously occupied the land. It's possible that the robed figure was just a spirit guide or might have been a former occupant that lived there before the house was built.

I did not realise at the time but our house was not very far from where the infamous Satanist and self-styled "Wickedest Man in the World" Aleister Crowley used to live. Netherwood was a guest house in the 1940s and the place Aleister Crowley died, in 1947. Although the house no longer exists Crowley's influence can still be felt in the area. I believe there are two ley lines that cross the area of my house, The Conquest Hospital and of course Netherwood. Perhaps Crowley was aware of this and it attracted him to the area.

Just off The Ridge there used to be an esoteric bookseller called Metaphysical Research Group or MRG for short. They dealt in reprints of rare esoteric manuscripts and other occult paraphernalia by mail order. There is an old story that Crowley entered into an occult battle with the founder of MRG; John J.J Williamson. Although I do not know if this is true or just an urban myth.

Hastings has attracted a wealth of artists, occultists and eccentrics over the years (Alex Sanders the famous witch lived and died there in 1988) The Infamous O.T.O also has a lodge in Hastings and the editor of the book The Necronomicon lived in the old town.

On the 26th October 2010, the Hastings Observer published a letter about bizarre things happening in two houses in Netherwood Close that were subsequently blessed. One thing I have since found is that to investigate Crowley; is to play with fire.

I met someone in MRG who I will refer to as G to protect his anonymity. G introduced me to the teachings of Louis Claude de St Martin, the founder of "Martinism" and esoteric Christianity and Theurgy (Angelic Magic). We have remained friends to this very day.

There was a rumour in Hastings that Crowley's ghost had been seen on the cliffs near the Castle in the 70s I believe. One night at 1am in the morning we set off on a ghost hunt around the Old Town in which it was said he used to frequent. Eventually we ended up on the cliffs searching by torchlight the precarious paths. Although we did not see Crowley's ghost there was definitely a feeling around the area of his dark presence.

Fast forward to 2013 and I found my interest in Crowley had been renewed through a series of strange coincidences and synchronicities.

This reminded me of my search years ago for the reports of his ghost being seen so as I placed an advertisement in the Hastings edition of the Friday Ad (a local free paper) requesting anyone with information on Crowley to contact me in confidence.

Not long after I received a phone-call from a withheld number from a well-spoken lady that knew Crowley personally! It turned out her father was a great friend of Crowley's and they used to write to each other. She had in her possession several letters between Crowley and her father and also items of furniture, as well as various personal belongings and artefacts of interest.

I concluded by the tone of her voice that she was of senior years. As Crowley passed away in 1947 I deduced she must be in her late 80s. She said Crowley was not a bit like the public persona so often portrayed, but actually highly intelligent, a great conversationalist and quite the opposite of "The Wickedest Man in The World"

We spoke for about fifteen minutes about my interest and she asked if she could call me again at some point. I asked for her number, which she would not give me. Instead she provided me with her family name which shall remain confidential. I shall refer to her as Mrs L.

Unfortunately, she did not get back in touch as I had hoped as I had many questions I wished to ask her about his life. I again placed an advert in the local paper asking Mrs L to contact me in confidence but alas to this day I have heard no more from her. I did some research based upon her surname and what she told me about her father. I discovered in his time he was quite famous for having a large collection of artefacts relating to folklore. But what happened next was even more bizarre.

The contact sparked my memory of Crowley in Hastings and I became almost obsessed with getting in touch with this woman. I found he invaded my thoughts and dreams daily and I couldn't get him out of my head. Each day something odd would happen, little things that make you think, odd smells, feelings, something seen but unseen was around me.

One morning I was walking through Canterbury, it was a bright clear day and I felt drawn to a solitary gentleman sitting on a bench smoking a pipe. There was no one else around and he was dressed in an odd manner, wearing clothes not suited to the modern day. I seemed to walk past him in slow motion as though time had stood still, as I glanced he looked at me and then turned away. As I walked past and turned back to look at him, he had vanished, nowhere to be seen. I swear to this day I had witnessed Crowley's ghost staring back at me

I was so disturbed by this vision I spent several hours looking up pictures of Crowley on the internet and to my shock I found the image that bore his likeness. The picture reproduced below is of the man I saw in broad daylight sitting on a bench that was there one minute gone the next.

I believe his influence lives on and if you search him out he will find you. I have had many unexplained "coincidences" concerning Crowley in my life, even before I moved to Hastings he had been at the back of my consciousness. So, to end this first chapter I will just say beware what you search for as you may just find it. Crowley had quite a disturbing effect on my consciousness and it took a long time to erase him and his presence from my life.

Aleister Crowley as I witnessed in Canterbury

Hastings Old Town

A Haunting in Scotland

My father passed away in 1993 and not long after we took a family vacation in Scotland to mourn his passing and have a break. My brother in law had booked two timeshare lodges near a Loch in the Highlands for us to share. In one was my sister, brother in law and her family and in the other my mother, wife, and myself.

The lodges were of a fairly modern design, built into the hillside. The only odd thing about them was the fact the lounge/dining room and kitchen were upstairs and the bedrooms and sauna downstairs. The lounge was open plan with a raised central area where there was a table and six chairs for dining.

We did all the usual things: sightseeing, walking, swimming etc. It was fairly uneventful for the first day or so. But then one night everything changed. We went to bed downstairs as usual myself with my wife in one room and my mother in the room next to ours. I tried to doze off but found myself slipping in and out of consciousness. At one point, I clearly heard a child's voice say "daddy". I sat up in bed and woke my wife who was fast asleep and asked her if she had heard it to which she replied, "no you must have been dreaming" and promptly went back to sleep.

I sat in bed with an ever-increasing feeling of dread, the darkness of the room seemed to engulf me as I kept hearing noises from upstairs. Little thumps, footsteps, creaks and groans. Once again, I closed my eyes only to immediately open them when I again I heard a child's voice say quite clearly "daddy". By now my heart was racing (even psychic mediums get nervous sometimes!) As I looked around the room the hairs on my arms stood up but I could see nothing to account for the ghostly voice. In due course, I went to sleep but had a very restless night of tossing and turning with disturbed dreams.

In the morning, my mother woke us with a knock on the door asking why I had come into her room last night. I explained I hadn't but she said the door opened, she heard footsteps and breathing and thought it was me messing about. I protested my innocence and she then said did I hear the noises upstairs? I said yes I did but I thought it was just the creaks and groans of the lodge. We went upstairs and to our absolute shock found the dining chairs had all been turned upside down! We really could not believe what we were seeing and all of us looked for a logical explanation but there was none.

By now we were all on edge and decided to go down to the main reception area to speak to someone about our experiences. A lady came out of reception and I opened the conversation by asking "Has anyone ever experienced anything in lodge xxx?" to which she gave a blank stare. I sensed there was something underlying her apparently blank expression so I pressed on "Has anything every happened there?"

This time she went back into the office and an older woman in her 60s came out. We explained what had happened and then she told us a few years ago two young girls had stayed in the room but refused to sleep there another night as they kept seeing dark shadows. So, they ended up sleeping in the games room on the snooker table!

I asked if anyone had died in the room to which she replied not to her knowledge. As we were all so unnerved by the experience, especially my mother we asked to change lodges. As there were none available we had to tell my sister about the events that had transpired. They listened intently, saying nothing but could tell by our reactions we were all a bit shook up so agreed to make up beds in their lodge on the floor for their children and we could bunk there.

That night we went to my sisters' lodge whilst my then wife went to our lodge to pick up a few of our clothes. She was gone quite some time so I went up to the lodge to see why she was taking so long. I arrived to find her sitting on the top of the stairs, white as a sheet, crying. I asked what was wrong and she said that when she was upstairs in the lounge she walked past the top of the stairs and had seen someone she thought was me pass by at the bottom. She then went downstairs but there was no one to be seen. She went back upstairs and heard footsteps, followed by our bedroom door close. As she approached the stairs she saw shadows moving out of the corner of her eye which frightened her as there was nothing to cause them.

That was it, we were out of there like a rocket. We never did discover if anything had happened there in the past, although we sensed the site owners knew more about the history of the place and our lodge in particular than they were letting on.

Strangely enough many years later I was to hear the child's voice say "daddy" again. More on that in a later chapter.

So, was it haunted? I think something was definitely there, I don't think it was dark or evil in any way it may just be a manifesting of psychic energy that was triggered by the obvious grief of losing my father. I cannot explain the voice or what my wife saw or the moving of the furniture, perhaps some soul just wanted us to know they were there?

Ghosts in the Cottage

In 2003 following the breakup of my marriage I moved into a 14th century idyllic cottage in the village of Hellingly, East Sussex. The cottage was quite quaint and located near to the church yard and had two upstairs bedrooms, a through kitchen/living room/dining room the length of the house and a tiny bathroom. It was the scene of the most paranormal activity I have experienced to date in my life.

During my time, there I kept a diary of the odd goings on which I reproduce in part here:

25/02/2003 - Woken by a tremendous crash from downstairs, sounds like a wardrobe had fallen over as the whole place shook. Crept downstairs at 2.44am with a torch, hope it's not burglars. Nothing there to account for noise – weird went back to bed.

18/07/2003 - Sitting downstairs on my computer writing in the dining room when I distinctly heard a child's voice say "daddy" over my right shoulder. I turned around expecting to see someone but no one was there. What's strange is this happened in Scotland in the 90s.

22/07/2003 - Woke up at 3am with a start saw a dark shape coming out of the wall, man like then it vanished – scary.

21/08/2003 - Tuesday evening after midnight thought I smelt incense, went to bed at 12.45 and smelt perfume in bedroom.

25/11/2003 - Very bad night sleep dreamt of a small dwarf like man who had black hair and close-cropped beard. He told me his name but I can't recall it, I think it begun with the letter H but it was unusual and short, he told me he was the guardian of something.

18/12/2003 - Very vivid dream last night, myself G and other healers and light workers were in a dark and evil place. Mountains, woods, castles etc. Very foreboding. We were climbing a mountain path to a hill fort, we went down to the other side of a wooded copse and became trapped by a group of people practicing black magic and Satanism. I saw someone I knew, JG and looked him in the eyes but he looked like a lost soul his eyes were lifeless.

There was an older lady in a black robe also a man who was the "master" or leader. SG was also there and had a plastic bag placed over his head with occult symbols on it and was suffocated as the others chanted. Chaos erupted and I attacked the attackers. I awoke with a start at 3.28am feeling very scared, sweating, very real dream.

(Footnote I mention this dream because as I was to learn the soul travels when we sleep to many strange places and learns lessons. This dream turned out to be a prophetic warning about a Black Magic group I

30

would come up against at a later date that worked over The Long Man of Wilmington chalk hill figure, and Littlington Church)

22/12/2003 - been dreaming a lot about evil or aspects of it, had a guide in my dream that put a headband on me with symbols on it as a form of psychic protection – Am I under psychic attack I wonder?

03/01/2004 - Awoke with a start at 2.30am the bed is actually shaking and vibrating with me in it! I'm not scared, think someone or something is trying to get my attention it lasted a few minutes then just stopped.
09/01/2004- Going to my girlfriends for a few days, can't sleep from the endless bangs and crashes in the night that wake me up. Strange smells and I hear whispered voices downstairs. Feel very uneasy, need a break.

18/02/2004 - Came across a book by "chance" except I know there are no chance happenings and everything is connected. The book by Franz Hartman called "With the Adepts" tells the story as an allegory of a mysterious dwarf that understands the dilemmas of the mind. I thought it relevant as it coincided with my previous dream about a dwarf.

24/04/2004 - Had some profound insights into the nature of reality following a deep meditation. God is mind/consciousness/energy, when the Bible says we are made in the image of God we have taken it literally. I believe/*know* it means on an inner emotional/thinking level our emotional/thinking level is God!

That's why we are ALL connected, life is a waking dream, and it's a dream within a dream. When we die our thinking/emotional level (energy) to join the group mind (God) taking with it all its earthly experiences, thereby enabling God to evolve.

Our concept of God, Heaven, and Hell is all wrong. God is closer than we think because we are ALL GOD, and by that we are all connected. Reality and everything in it are all an illusion. And by everything, I mean including religions. Everything is made from energy condensed into matter. When the Buddha was enlightened not only did he see the world was an illusion, but he saw the true nature that underlines it. By that, his fear was removed as he realised the world had no hold over him. Also, what we think we are we are, we attract to us what we think because thoughts are all part of that God energy.

Even our concept of time is an illusion, time as we perceive it does not exist. Everything happens in the same instant. We are all divine sparks from the creator, in shattered vessels experiencing ourselves.

All knowledge of a spiritual nature *must be* gained by *direct experience*. Nobody can tell you, you must not believe what you are told or read in books, you must test it, probe it, explore it yourself. Then you will discover the truth of our nature and of Gods.

When we go to sleep at night we wake up from the dream. Our souls travel freely.

God=Mind=Emotions=Thought It's amazing, our concept of Heaven and Hell are emotional/mental states.

The emerald tablet of Hermes, mentions "Nous" the infinite mind. The Knights Templar worshiped a head, Baphomet – Sophia – WISDOM. I believe it was just a representation of the mind, of consciousness represented by a head. They had a secret knowledge of our reality.

04/04/2004 - Woken again by whispering voices coming out of the walls, can't make out what they are saying though. Decided to talk to them to see if they would reply, they did! I asked who it was and was told a spirit, I said a prayer and tried to send it on its way.

I saw a child in the spare room and had thoughts and images flow into my mind of things that had happened in the cottage over the years. I was shown a fire that had happened a long time ago and trapped the family and killed them. It started in the fireplace downstairs (not the existing one) I stood at the bottom of the stairs and had a vision of a man/woman/child trapped by the smoke.

I believe the child died and her name was "Debbie" as I was shown it being carved into one of the beds. Then I kept being shown different events from the past, people coming and going, open fields, someone

33

coming who did not feel right. I felt a bit apprehensive, after a while the vision stopped and I went back to bed.

16/06/2004 - Did spiritual healing on a female client, witnessed a ball of blue light above her head.
28/07/2004- Cottage felt very strange today I kept sensing things. My clairvoyance and psychic senses seem to have opened up big time, I felt my Dad around me. There was an almighty crash in the kitchen that scared the shit out of me, no idea what caused it.

29/07/2004 - Witnessed an apparition in the cottage. Was downstairs reading when the atmosphere seemed to change and grow colder? I saw a floating, luminous mass in the dining room that just floated into view. I asked what it was and had the mental impression it was a form of spiritual energy that existed off humans but we were not aware of it consciously. The whole universe was alive with intelligent energies but most humans were not aware of them.

12/08/2004 - Did meditation up until 12.30am and managed to get into a deep trance state and then unexpectedly opened my eyes as the atmosphere in the room changed. I saw someone sitting on the bed beside me, a figure, not scared, then it just dissolved.

18/08/2004 - Was woken at 2.20am by the Suffolk latch on my bedroom door going up and down rapidly as though someone or something wants to come in. I

34

opened it tentatively, always cautious it may be burglars but no one there. I can't get back to sleep and feel like a dark energy has pervaded the place. It is very late but I ring my girlfriend as I feel very on edge I decide to drive to hers and arrive at 4.30 in the morning.

22/08/2004 - Dawn, her son and jenny came down, we went to the pub and found Jenny foaming at the mouth, eyes bulging like she was petrified of something. She had tried to chew her way through the dining room door in fear of something unseen.

23/08/2004 - Dawns son slept downstairs on the sofa but woke us in the night as he was scared. He said he kept seeing dark shapes and hearing voices.

27/08/2004 - I was doing housework during the day when suddenly the music on the Hi Fi blared out at full volume from the living room. It made me jump, I went into the room to find it had been turned up from 8 to 20! How? Who? I turned it down and nothing else occurred until that night.

I went to bed around midnight but was woken at 1.45am by muffled voices coming from downstairs. My first thought was burglars as where I lived was pretty isolated, I grabbed my heavy Maglite just in case and crept downstairs, there was nothing there (thank God) I wonder who or what is trying to communicate?

These are just a few of the many events I encountered in the cottage, the place itself did not have a bad feeling about it, but everyone that came there felt or witnessed something. I did some research into the history of the cottage but could find nothing to account for the paranormal phenomena I encountered there.

A Seance in Brighton

I have always been interested in all aspects of the paranormal and have longed to attend a Physical Séance. As chance would have it I noticed an advert in the local free paper about a circle near Brighton which was demonstrating Physical Phenomena in the séance room. Guests were invited by appointment for £8 so I rang up and expressed my interest. This is what occurred on 8/04/2004.

I arrived at the modern detached house to be greeted by the host. There were three other guests plus myself. A guy called Bob, a young couple and a developing medium who I recently discovered now holds his own physical séances. The regular sitters comprised a man in his 60s in whose house we were holding the séance, Barbara who invited me, the medium, a tall blonde French lady who was his doorkeeper, another guy and his American wife. The séance was held in a converted attic where all natural light was blacked out, it was illuminated by a single red light bulb.

We sat in a circle and I was placed directly in front of the medium, in the centre of the circle was a small round table with four legs, on the table was a cone and underneath was a very large stone, some crystal clusters, a tambourine, a harmonica and other bits and pieces.

We were all given a yellow daffodil to hold (I don't know why) we then joined hands and said the Lord's Prayer and were given a short speech on spiritual philosophy. During this, the medium who had his hands on his lap gently rocked backwards and forwards as he went into trance. After a while a spirit entranced the medium and addressed me and I was told about my healing and teaching work. Next a guide called Neil came through and spoke about my loving kindness and compassion for others. Then a very camp sounding guy called Marcus came through as direct voice. Finally, an old man with a heavy raspy voice told me of the power I possessed from previous incarnations, how I was a powerful healer/psychic/magician and would help others as a healer and teacher.

The red light was then turned off and we sat in pitch darkness, it was so black you literally could not see your hands in front of your face. The small table that had luminous bands attached to its legs started to shake as did the trumpet on top which also had luminous bands attached to it. Slowly the table began to creep towards me inch by inch which was quite fascinating to watch but also slightly unnerving in the pitch darkness of the séance room.

Suddenly the trumpet shot up into the air followed by the levitating table! Both clearly seen by the illuminated bands. It moved incredibly quickly around the room flying just above our seated heads within the confines of the circle of sitters. Its speed increased, it was moving so fast it was now a blur and I was surprised it hadn't hit anyone's heads as it was so close. The trumpet fell to the ground slowly and the table ended up upturned in the lap of the old man next to me.

During the levitations, the young guy that was seated to my left and was a visiting medium in training was proclaiming "The trumpets above my head, my glasses are being taken off, I'm being touched"

I also had a heavy crystal cluster drop into my lap which made me jump as I was not expecting it, the crystals felt very warm to the touch. When the red light was turned back on and we could see each other again, the medium was still seated opposite me and a young lady said she had water splashed over her, and the young man's glasses were the other side of the room. Everyone else was still seated.

The séance was certainly interesting to witness as it posed many questions, the most obvious being trickery. I have a strong interest in magic of the entertainment type and have performed as a semi-professional magician so I am fully aware of how it could have been faked. No matter how I analysed it I could not see how it was possible for the table to move in a pitch black room without knocking someone's head off! There is a possibility that the medium himself stood up when the light was extinguished and moved the table himself but he would have needed either a torch or night vision goggles to see anything. Also, the séance room was quite small with not a lot of clearance between the roof and your head. It would have been impossible, in my opinion, for it to have moved as fast as it did by human hands. Not only was it going around and around the circle at a tremendous speed, it was also revolving on its axis as it did so.

It would be possible for the medium to move the table with his foot towards me as he was seated directly opposite, and the great Harry Houdini shows this method in one of his famous exposes on fake mediums. But I do not think this was the case. I left the séance, my mind buzzing with both excitement at what I had witnessed but also doubts about certain aspects of the entity's that controlled the medium which I will elaborate on later. I decided to tell my girlfriend Dawn about the experience and see if it was possible to attend again. Dawn is very level headed and not prone to flights of fancy and I wanted a second witness to see if I had missed the obvious.

17/05/2004 - As luck would have it we managed to get a second invite to another demonstration with Dawn as my guest. As she is a natural sceptic, very logical in her thought processes and didn't suffer fools gladly I thought she would be ideal to spot any trickery. Plus, with my own experience and interest in the ways of the magician, I knew what to look out for.

My own thoughts were that Dawn would think it a load of bollocks but the night proved interesting and thought provoking. We both witnessed a small child darting around the small cramped circle under red light

40

conditions, and there was a distinct drop in temperature when the manifestation started. Several spirits came through the medium almost immediately, once again I was told I should be doing more healing work so this time I took it on board. We both witnessed the table spinning around above our heads incredibly fast again and also direct voice coming above our heads some way from the medium, lights were also in abundance.

Conclusions

If the séance was faked, and I really do not believe it was then what was the motive? Certainly not financial as they only took £8 per guest, about £32. Then there was the cost of advertising it in the local paper plus tea and cakes were provided afterwards and the balance would have to be split six ways.

The Medium

Was he deliberately fooling the others? Or was he the subject of multiple personality disorder and not aware of it himself? There have been many documented cases of untrained mediums being "taken over" by playful spirits that have tricked both the medium and the sitters into believing they were someone else. These negative entity's feed off of the group energy and are like parasites and can cause real emotional and psychological problems to the unaware. When the medium went into trance and came through as the old man with a rasping, gurgling voice had he secretly taken a swig of water? This may explain one of the sitters saying she got sprayed with water, possibly on purpose or accident?

Were the Whole Group Being Deceived?

Were the group being deceived? Were they blind to the truth as they had their own beliefs and desires to witness and communicate with spirit?

Several Questions

How did the table levitate and move? When it first started to vibrate and move I was directly facing the seated medium in total darkness. It would have been possible for him to push it with his feet while remaining seated and holding hands or tied to the chair. Or, he could have had an accomplice sitting next to him, either the gatekeeper who was the French lady or the American lady. All attention would be on the medium so through misdirection the accomplice could possibly have moved the table on the floor.

When the table levitated above our heads someone could have stood up unseen in the darkness and lifted them up. However, it was so dark that they could not see anything unless they had night vision goggles or more than one of them was in on it. I was suspicious of the American lady and her husband and also the young trainee medium as they all sat closely together.

Why can't the manifestation appear in red light?

Maybe the motivation is simply fame and knowing you are fooling people?

Or, did I witness the impossible, something wonderful and unexplainable by rational means? Did some energy manifested by the sitters move items? I would have been more convinced if I had received some very personal, precise information about myself and dead relatives.

I would have been happier if we had all retained hand contact throughout and the medium was fully restrained and the restraints were examined by myself. After much thought I have come to the following possible conclusion.

1.   The table really did move but spirits did not do it. It was as yet some form of energy generated by the sitters as yet unexplained by science. Similar to poltergeist activity, perhaps generated through the sub-conscious mind by wish fulfilment and emotion.

2.   The medium is unintentionally deceiving himself and others that "spirits" talk through him. It's just aspects of his own sub-conscious personality or as Carl Jung said, "The Collective Unconscious"

3.   It was an experiment to see how people could be fooled by what they saw through suggestion. The big question maybe is not how, but why?

4.   My gut feeling says it was genuine but the medium was subject to a negative entity that fed off the expectations of both the medium and the sitters. One of the personalities that came through the medium insisted upon being referred to as "Sir" which is very autocratic and dominant. I felt uneasy about this from the start and after reading through the blog the Circle uses to publish online I felt they were being used by negative energy entities.

I think this is a case you can make your own conclusions from. I have gone into it in some detail for two reasons: Firstly, to highlight what happens at a Physical Séance which is something quite rare to witness first hand these days without forking out hundreds of pounds. Secondly as a warning to mediums and would be mediums and sitters about the danger of being overshadowed by negative life forms. Believe me it does happen and I have witnessed it many times in my lifetime.

As far as I am aware the Circle has disbanded. I did try to track down some of the people that attended but had no luck. The website with the blog has been taken down, but I did discover quite by chance that the young trainee medium that had his glasses removed is now a full time Physical Medium. I will not reveal his name as he has had mixed reviews in the psychic press as to his séances, but as soon as I read a report of one of them I knew it was the same person.

Dangers of the Ouija – A Warning for the Curious

Many people have an interest in Ghosts, the Paranormal and The Occult. The mysterious hidden part of life has always provided a fascination for mankind. Our ancient ancestors communicated with spirits whilst in deep drug induced trance states. The South American Shaman communicate with the spirits of nature. And up and down the country in spiritualist churches many go in search of truth and answers and hopefully a message from a departed love one.

One of the forms of communication that temps many is that of The Ouija board, and here is a true life cautionary tale I call "Dangers of the Ouija – A warning for the curious"

"Ouija board would you work for me I have got to get through to a good friend" go the lyrics of the Morrissey song. The Ouija board, also known as the Spirit board or the Talking board is a flat board marked with the letters of the alphabet, the numbers 0-9, and the words Yes/No and goodbye along with various graphics. It is a registered trademark of Hasbro Inc. that market it as a board game!

It uses a small heart-shaped piece of wood or movable indicator to point to letters of the alphabet by spelling out the spirits message during a séance. Participants place their fingers lightly on the indicator and it moves around the board seemingly under its own power. Parapsychology suggests that the board works by using unconscious micro muscle movements from the sitter's fingertips- in other words they move it themselves, unconsciously, spelling out words and messages from the "deceased". The technical term is Ide Motor Response and it is thought dowsing pendulums work in a similar way.

My first experience of an Ouija board came at secondary school when four of us used an upturned glass as the pointer and wrote letters of the alphabet on scraps of paper. We each touched one finger lightly on the glass and asked if anyone was there. Almost immediately the glass moved over our desktop to spell "Yes". Nervous with the excitement of youth we went ahead each assuring the other we were not moving or pushing it ourselves. To test it, one of the lads (David) removed his finger and asked if anyone knew his mother's maiden name (we didn't). The three of us remaining then placed our fingers on the glass and asked the question "what is David's mother's maiden name?" To our surprise it then began to spell out her name correctly, a name we didn't know.

This whetted our appetite and David once again joined our circle and we continued to ask various questions. But then suddenly without warning the glass seemed to take on a life of its own, moving faster and faster and very erratically it shot here and there but did not make sense so we all removed our fingers and it came to a standstill. After a discussion among ourselves we tried again to make contact and placed our fingertips on the glass.

David asked, "Is there anyone there?" to which the glass again answered "Yes". "Are you male or female?" the glass answered "male". We then asked its name to which it started to move to spell; A -D -O -L - F - H -I -T - L - E -R! This scared us so much we stopped immediately, each not sure it was a joke played by one of the others, but it shook us all enough not to try it again.

It was not until 1992 that I came into contact with Ouija boards again and the inherent danger they have. This is a true story of obsession, blackmail, Satanism, and possession. I have changed the names of the people involved to protect those still living.

Martin was a family friend, working at an Asylum in mid Kent as a store man. I had known him for several years and he was aware of my interest and experience in the paranormal and occult. During those days, I worked as a sales rep and used to pop in to see him for a cup of tea and a chat when I was in the area. He was married with two grown up children, living near Maidstone.

I knew Martin's wife very well and on occasion had Sunday lunch with them. Martin's wife Sally confided in me on the quiet that she was worried about him as he was acting strangely and suspiciously. She had suspicions he was having an affair to which I replied don't be ridiculous. She was convinced something was going on as he was becoming more and more distant

48

and vague, he used to disappear for days at a time with no explanation of where he went.

Several weeks went by and one evening Sally rang me in tears to say Martin had been seen getting into a car with a young girl who she knew worked at the Asylum. She had heard rumours that he was having an affair with her. Martin was in his late fifties at the time and the girl in question was in her late twenties, so to me it seemed unbelievable he would risk his twenty plus years of marriage.

Sally managed to follow Martin one evening when he said he was going to the pub. He in fact met with the girl and two others in a car and drove off. When Sally questioned Martin that evening he assured her all was well and the girl and the others were just friends. He claimed they had a shared interest in ghost hunting and he was joining them on a hunt. However, Sally found this odd, as Martin had never mentioned this interest before!

A month went by and during this time Martin upped and left Sally with no explanation except that he was in love with somebody else. Sally, distraught and angry, started divorce proceedings. Two weeks after Martin left he turned up out of the blue looking dishevelled, tired and incoherent. He was babbling a story about getting involved with a group that practiced black magic, drug taking, sex, demons and god knows what.

Sally contacted me and I came over to find Martin looking a right state, he had aged in the short time since I had seen him last and his eyes were dulling and soulless. I started to question Martin into what was going on and he said he was having trouble recollecting some of it as it seemed like a dream and so far-fetched we would not believe it. He told us that the girl he worked with had developed a fixation with him and he liked the attention coming from a young girl. After some screaming from Sally I said it might be better if they discuss this between themselves as there was obviously a lot of issues to sort out and it was probably personal.

I left them to it and the next day Sally called me to say she was at her wit's end as Martin had come out with this incredible story about black magic, Ouija boards and "entity's". She thought it was either bullshit or he was losing his mind. I got in touch with Martin at work and arranged to meet him. We met in a lay by and sat in the car talking. He told me the girl at work used to flirt with him which flattered his ego. This led on to her inviting him to have a go with an Ouija board. He became intrigued when the board started to give personal information that she could not know about his past and his family. He became hooked, addicted as he put it and at first treated it as harmless fun with an attractive girl.

One day she kissed him and this lead on to a sexual relationship of sorts. They continued to meet when they could. She then invited him to meet some people in Brighton she thought he would be interested in. It turned out these "friends" ran a ritualistic magic group, he was invited to attend a meeting as her guest and his curiosity tempted, he went along.

During the meeting drinks flowed freely, there were about a dozen or so people there of mixed sexes and various ages. He was given some tablets that they said would give him a wonderful experience and being both gullible and suggestible, he took them. Martin then went very strange on me; his eyes looked full of fear as though he was reliving the experience. He told me he couldn't remember all the details but he remembers they started to carry out some sort of chanting and then a ritual of some sort. The young girl undressed and the men in the group caressed her, she then laid on the altar they'd set up and a man in a gold mask dis-robed and had sex with her whilst they all watched. Martin said he was both repulsed and turned on by this at the same time. The drink and possible drugs made everything seem like a dream as though he was not actually there.

Martin was then invited to make love with her, which he did. More chanting followed and the air was thick with incense and what smelt like cannabis smoke but he was unsure. He then looked terrified as he told me that a small hideous statue that was placed upon the altar came to life and started to move. He said he saw demons in the room. I suspect he was hallucinating, brought upon by the drink, drugs and atmosphere, but who knows for sure?

He was terrified he said because he could not remember the rest, he tried to end the relationship but said he couldn't as he felt compelled to keep going back to her. At night, he often dreamt she was calling him in his sleep. With that, he abruptly stopped and said he had told me too much already, he made his excuses and left. To be honest I didn't know what to think. Martin was always a bit gullible to say the least, but this was just unbelievable. As events turned out it was more real and more terrifying than I initially realised and it took all my and Martins strength to break free from the group. To cut a long story short I am going to jump forward now.

Martin found himself becoming obsessed with the group; he was being blackmailed with compromising photos. That the group threatened showing his wife if he tried to leave, so he continued with the "relationship" with the girl. At one point Sally phoned me about 21.45 to say Martin had gone missing and had mumbled about going to Devils Dyke (a hill near Brighton). She begged me to drive over there to see if I could see him so I picked up Sally's daughter and we drove over to Devils Dyke. I pulled over into a lay by and we got out of the car, it was dark and cold so I left the car headlights on and got my torch out. It was eerily quiet, we looked around and found a small area that had the remains of a very small fire as it was scorched. There were also the remains of black candle wax which seemed odd, but no sign of Martin.

I had friends in a Rosicrucian group that were light workers, did healing and exorcisms that I turned to for help. They had some experience in helping people

52

escape cults and also combating black magic groups. I urged Martin to contact them for his sanity and his marriage as he was becoming more and more distant, depressed, moody and withdrawn. They managed to help him after literally holding him captive in a secluded farmhouse in Wiltshire.

There he was cared for and it transpired that the group used sex as a threat to attract and keep members. He had been targeted as he was very suggestible and once he was given the pills they used hypnosis on him. This altered state made him see "demons" and a post hypnotic suggestion was planted that when a black candle was burned and a keyword given he would be compelled to attend.

I helped with the Hypnosis as some years before I was trained in Hypnotherapy for my own self development, many years later I ended up as a highly successful Hypnotherapist in private practice in Harley Street with a senior qualification in Hypnotherapy practice.

I became subject to psychic attacks myself and have no doubt this was a serious black magic group not just in it for kicks. Martin's initial attraction and introduction by playing with the Ouija opened a doorway to his sub-conscious for more thrills. This is how these groups work; they lure you in with promises of sex, money, power, magic, and then you're hooked and it's too late. You're kept in place through blackmail as photos are taken of you in compromising positions, and you are dragged into a web of darkness until there is no limit to the depths of depravity you will sink.

Black Magic and Satanic groups exist, have no doubt, and Sussex is a hotbed. If you doubt this read Toyne Newton's excellent expose of Satanism in Sussex, "The Demonic Connection". Martin's marriage broke up and Sally passed away from natural causes. I haven't seen or heard from Martin in years. The last I learnt he had remarried and moved to Cornwall.

The Asylum is no more as when care into community came into being it was closed down. The group still exists and as far as I am aware now operates from several different areas of Sussex. I came up against them again about 2003/4 as they were using Wilmington Hill as it lies on a natural ley line. This may sound nonsense, this may sound like make-believe but I cannot stress enough the dangers of being lured into the dark occult through something as simple and innocent as an Ouija board game.

Darkness and evil exists my friends, and there are followers of darkness as there are followers, like myself and others, of light. And where there is light there is darkness, and the light flickers like a flame on the lower astral attracting darkness like moths to a flame. For there is no light without dark, no dark without light. You do not need to know secret rituals in order to invoke the powers of darkness.

Transfiguration

This is only a brief extract of the more interesting experiences from my paranormal diary's but hardly a week goes by when something has not happened that is unexplainable by rational means.

As part of my continuing unfoldment I meditate most days and I give private psychic readings and healing to those in need. It is often during these "atonements" that something of a paranormal nature happens, minds are still and we are in tune with the hidden realms that surround us

On 22nd January 1992, I was in deep conversation with a good friend when I felt myself starting to go off as the conversation was going on at a bit of a drone, as I mentally switched off but feigned interest in what she was saying her face began to mist over and her features began to change. Firstly, into that of my deceased father, then my aunt Wendy who had died at the far too young age of 45 from lung cancer followed by an old woman with a bun in her air that appeared to be knitting? I sort of watched this happen in a kind of trance and then suddenly snapped out of it, as my consciousness returned to everyday reality the faces vanished and once again I was staring at my friend in slight disbelief!

My mother mentioned to me on the 30th January 1992 that my father had spoken to her and she had felt his presence around. When I described my experience with my friend she immediately recognised the old lady with a bun as her mothers, mother describing her perfectly. The following day we had an Asian couple round our house to discuss babysitting our children, as we sat there conversing I once again felt myself being disassociated and "going off" into limbo, and to my surprise once again I experienced the same transfiguration of the man's face this time into an old man with beard and hair.

This "face changing" has happened on several occasions and I used to have a Jewish High Priest come through that was one of my spirit guides, this fellow had a very powerful but serene presence, worse a headdress with a breastplate with twelve stones, he looked like he had stepped out of a biblical epic by Cecil B De Mile! Every so often he pops up in my life either during a Psychic reading or to impart teaching and higher knowledge to me.

I sat in a Spiritualist development circle in 2013 and it was during one of these circles that a new guide introduced himself to me. It was decided by the circle leader Matt, a jovial Irishman and Medium himself that I would act as the medium on this occasion. WE all sat holding hands and I said a small prayer and gave a short philosophical speech. Straightaway I was aware of this presence which manifested itself an incredible heat and power. I heard a door open and close and footsteps and as I had my eyes closed in meditation asked if anyone had left or come into the room. The gatekeeper said no one had.

I had this impression of this figure pulsating with white light and immense energy, his aura was so strong the others in the circle could physically feel the heat. He gave us various personal messages then taught us some philosophical higher truths before departing. His name was Jonas and he is with me to this day.

Jonas, my healing guide.

Printed in Great Britain
by Amazon